Eeyore's
Little Book of
Gloom

Inspired by A.A. Milne & Illustrated by E.H. Shepard

This edition first published in Great Britain 1999
for The Book People Ltd, Hall Wood Avenue,
Haydock, St Helens WA11 9UL
by Egmont Children's Books Limited
239 Kensington High Street, London W8 6SA
Copyright © 1999 Michael John Brown, Peter Janson-Smith,
Roger Hugh Vaughan Charles Morgan and Timothy Michael Robinson,
Trustees of the Pooh Properties.
Adapted from *Winnie-the-Pooh*, *The House at Pooh Corner*
and *Now We Are Six*
text by A.A. Milne and line illustrations by E.H. Shepard
copyright under the Berne Convention
Devised by Charlie Gardner
Book design by Philip Powell
copyright © 1999 Egmont Children's Books Limited
ISBN 1 85613 616 7

1 3 5 7 9 10 8 6 4 2

Printed in Hong Kong

"Nobody minds. Nobody cares. Pathetic, that's what it is."

When We Were Very Glum

Eeyore, the old grey Donkey, is sadder than ever. When I explained to him that I needed to write a *Foreword* to this book, Eeyore said that he would rather have a *Backword*, at the end of the volume, because, as Eeyore said, "Everybody knows that people in Bookshops and Whatnots simply read the last page of the book so that they don't have to buy it — How Like Them!" And he humped off.

And so, gentle reader, with that suitably cynical and doleful declaration still ringing in my ears, it is with great sadness that I commend to you this truly miserable collection. The best of the worst of Eeyore's

melancholia (including all the leftovers and the bits that got trodden on) in one Meagre Manual that will be read once and then never seen again — except perhaps as a wedge to level a Wobbly Table or suchlike. Well, as Eeyore says: "It's just what *would* happen."

Be Honest about your Feelings

"And how are you?" said Winnie-the-Pooh. Eeyore shook his head from side to side. "Not very how," he said. "I don't seem to have felt at all how for a long time."

Eeyore's Second Law of Motion.

A falling Pooh Bear will land
on a gorse bush, but ...

... a falling Tigger will land on an Eeyore!

Make First Impressions Count

"What did you say it was?" he asked.
"Tigger."
"Ah!" said Eeyore.
"He's just come," explained Piglet.
"Ah!" said Eeyore again.
He thought for a long time and then said:
"When is he going?"

Two Steps Forward?

If you follow you own footsteps ... you'll only find the road to nowhere.

A True Friend ...

will desert you in your time of need!

Politeness costs NOTHING!

"Good morning, Little Piglet," said Eeyore. "If it *is* a good morning," he said. "Which I doubt," said he. "Not that it matters," he said.

"How Like Them"

Even if you think you have nothing
worth stealing ...

someone will come along and take your tail.

Inflexible Problem Solving

What's gone is gone ...

whichever way you look at it.

The Wrong Answers

are the ones you go looking for when the right
answer is staring you in the face.

Invisible Mending

You can give the donkey a happy ending ...

but the miserable beginning remains forever.

$E = H_2O$

You can lead a horse to water ...

but you can't make him sink!

Disparage Success

But Eeyore was saying to himself, "This writing business. Pencils and what-not. Over-rated, if you ask me. Silly stuff. Nothing in it."

Make Depression your Friend

"I might have known," said Eeyore. "After all, one can't complain. I have my friends. Somebody spoke to me only yesterday. And was it last week or the week before that Rabbit bumped into me and said 'Bother!' The Social Round. Always something going on."

Gaze on Greyness

Cultivate a permanently tragic
expression by staring at your reflection
for hours on end; it's sure to bring a touch
of gloom to even the sunniest of days.

*Aaacent*uate the Negative

"Why, what's the matter?"
"Nothing, Pooh Bear, nothing. We can't all, and some of us don't. That's all there is to it. … I'm not complaining, but There It Is."

*Eeelimi*nate the Positive

"That's right," said Eeyore. "Sing. Umty-tiddly,
umty-too. Here we go gathering Nuts and May.
Enjoy yourself."
"I am," said Pooh.
"Some can," said Eeyore.

Pretend it's your Birthday Party

"Sad? Why should I be sad? It's my birthday.
The happiest day of the year."
"Your birthday?" said Pooh in great surprise.
"Of course it is. Can't you see? Look at all the
presents I have had."
"Presents?" said Pooh. "*Where?*"
"Can't you see them?"

"No," said Pooh.
"Neither can I," said Eeyore.
"Joke," he explained. "Ha ha!"

1.

2.

3.

4.

Invent a Gloomy Game

Ask a "friend" to *bounce* you into the river and then contemplate your greyness as you float downstream. Get another "friend" to shock you back to reality by dropping rocks on you as you float under a bridge – just for *fun*, of course.

Lose your Friendships

Avoid unexpected guests "dropping in" by placing your door knocker just out of reach.

Offer Destructive Criticism

"I'm giving this to Eeyore," he explained,
"as a present. What are *you* going to give?"
"Couldn't I give it too?" said Piglet,
"from both of us?"
"No," said Pooh. "That would *not*
be a good plan."

Expect the Worst

Even if someone remembers to come to your
birthday party, they will almost certainly ...

eat your present on the way ...

or break it!

Write Down your Worries

And then depress your companions by reading
them out loud.

Enjoy Boredom

It's all you've got to look forward to.

Try Group Therapy

"It's bad enough," said Eeyore, almost breaking down, "being miserable myself, what with no presents and no cake and no candles, and no proper notice taken of me at all, but if everybody else is going to be miserable too —"

Be a Begrudging Team Player

"What I say," said Eeyore, "is that it's unsettling. I didn't want to come on this Expo — what Pooh said. I only came to oblige. ... But if, every time I want to sit down for a little rest, I have to brush away half a dozen of Rabbit's smaller friends-and-relations first, then this isn't an Expo -- whatever it is — at all, it's simply a Confused Noise. That's what I say."

Limit your Liability

"All right," said Eeyore. "We're going. Only
Don't Blame Me."

Life is a Box of Thistles ...

and I've been dealt all the really
tough and prickly ones.

Resist Enthusiasm

"I'm not asking anybody," said Eeyore. "I'm just telling everybody. We can look for the North Pole, or we can play 'Here we go gathering Nuts and May' with the end part of an ants' nest. It's all the same to me."

Damn with Faint Praise

"Pooh's found the North Pole," said
Christopher Robin. "Isn't that lovely?"
"Is that it?" said Eeyore.
"Yes," said Christopher Robin.
"Is that what we were looking for?"
"Yes," said Pooh.
"Oh!" said Eeyore. "Well, anyhow —
it didn't rain," he said.

Visualise a Thunderstorm

It's just what *would* happen!

Turn a Deaf Ear to Good News

"Eeyore," said Owl,
"Christopher Robin is giving a party."
"Very interesting," said Eeyore. "I suppose they
will be sending me down the odd bits which got
trodden on. Kind and Thoughtful. Not at all,
don't mention it."

Be a Miserable Big Head

"It's much better than mine," said Pooh
admiringly, and he really thought it was.
"Well," explained Eeyore modestly,
"it was meant to be."

Staring into the Pit of Despair.

Expect to be Interrupted

"AS – I – WAS – SAYING," said Eeyore loudly
and sternly, "as I was saying when I was
interrupted by various Loud Sounds …"

Don't Expect Gratitude – Ask For It!

"If anybody wants to clap,"
said Eeyore when he had read this,
"now is the time to do it."
They all clapped.
"Thank you," said Eeyore.
"Unexpected and gratifying,
if a little lacking in Smack."

Be Positively Negative

Piglet explained to Tigger that he mustn't mind what Eeyore said because he was *always* gloomy; and Eeyore explained to Piglet that, on the contrary, he was feeling particularly cheerful this morning.

Master Miserable Meteorology

"It's snowing still," said Eeyore gloomily.
"So it is."
"*And* freezing."
"Is it?"
"Yes," said Eeyore. "However," he said,
brightening up a little, "we haven't had an
earthquake lately."

Play it DOWN!

"What's the matter, Eeyore?"
"Nothing, Christopher Robin. Nothing
important. I suppose you haven't seen
a house or what-not anywhere about?"
"What sort of a house?"
"Just a house."
"Who lives there?"

"I do. At least I thought I did. But I suppose I
don't. After all, we can't all have houses."

Seek Attention in the Gloom

"And I said to myself: The others will be sorry
if I'm getting myself all cold. They haven't got
Brains, any of them, only grey fluff that's blown
into their heads by mistake, and they don't
Think, but if it goes on snowing for another six
weeks or so, one of them will begin to say to
himself: 'Eeyore can't be so very much too Hot

about three o'clock in the morning.' And
then it will Get About. And they'll be Sorry."

Sharpen your Bluntness

"I've got a sort of idea," said Pooh at last,
"but I don't suppose it's a very good one."
"I don't suppose it is either," said Eeyore.

Make your Friends Come to You

"Nobody tells me," said Eeyore. "Nobody keeps me informed. I make it seventeen days come Friday since anybody spoke to me."
"It's your fault, Eeyore. You've never been to see any of us. You just stay here in this one corner of the Forest waiting for the others to come to *you*. Why don't you go to *them* sometimes?"

Accept Defeat Disgracefully

"He *knew*? You mean this A thing is a thing *Rabbit* knew?"

"Yes, Eeyore. He's clever, Rabbit is."

"Clever!" said Eeyore scornfully, putting a foot heavily on his three sticks. "Education!" said Eeyore bitterly, jumping on his six sticks. "What is Learning?" asked Eeyore as he kicked his twelve sticks into the air. "A thing *Rabbit* knows! Ha!"

Double Whammy

No matter how bad things seem …

... nothing could be worse than
being used as a towel rail.

Ignore the *Small* Print

"Hallo, Eeyore," he said,
"what are you looking for?"
"Small, of course," said Eeyore.
"Haven't you any brain?"
"Oh, but didn't I tell you?" said Rabbit.
"Small was found two days ago."
There was a moment's silence. "Ha-ha," said

Eeyore bitterly. "Merriment and what-not.
Don't apologize. It's just what *would* happen."

End on a Negative

"There is an invitation for you." …
"Ah!" said Eeyore. "A mistake, no doubt,
but still, I shall come.
Only don't blame *me* if it rains."

Leave them Wanting Less

"Everybody crowds round so in this Forest. There's no Space. I never saw a more Spreading lot of animals in my life, and all in the wrong places. Can't you *see* that Christopher Robin wants to be alone? I'm going." And he humped off.

Things ...

... can only get wetter!

A.A. MILNE

A.A. Milne, born in 1882, had already made his name as a dramatist and novelist when *Winnie-the-Pooh* was published in 1926. Milne's stories about Winnie-the-Pooh were written for his son Christopher Robin. The characters in the stories were based upon the real nursery toys which belonged to Christopher Robin, and their adventures are set in the Ashdown Forest where the family lived. The wise words in this little book are to be found in A.A. Milne's books, *Winnie-the-Pooh* and *The House at Pooh Corner.*

E.H. SHEPARD

E. H. Shepard became known as 'The man who drew Pooh'. Born in 1879, Shepard was able to draw well from a very young age. He won a scholarship to the Royal Academy of Arts and became acclaimed as an artist and illustrator. E.H. Shepard's witty and affectionate illustrations of Pooh and his friends from the Hundred Acre Wood are an inseparable part of the appeal of the stories. His illustrations for *Winnie-the-Pooh* and *The House at Pooh Corner* have become classics, recognised all over the world.